A GIFT

just for you

To:

From:

I shall not fear for I trust in the Lord.
He will comfort and protect me.

Psalm 23
A Psalm of David

The Lord is my shepherd

I SHALL NOT WANT

He maketh me to lie down in green pastures

He leadeth me
beside the still waters

He restoreth my soul

He leadeth me in the paths of righteousness for his name's sake

Yea. though I walk through the valley of
the shadow of death

I WILL FEAR NO EVIL

For thou art with me

Thy rod and thy staff they comfort me

Thou preparest a table before me in the presence of mine enemies

Thou anointest my head with oil

My cup runneth over

Surely goodness and mercy shall follow me all the days of my life

mercy

And I will dwell in the
house of the Lord

Forever

www.ingramcontent.com/pod-product-compliance
Lightning Source LLC
Chambersburg PA
CBHW042010110726
48006CB00004B/1035